Broken for a Purpose

Broken for a Purpose

By Michael Bacon

XULON PRESS

Xulon Press
2301 Lucien Way #415
Maitland, FL 32751
407.339.4217
www.xulonpress.com

Scripture quotations taken from the King James Version (KJV)–*public domain.*

Printed in the United States of America.

ISBN-13: 9781545656600

Table of Contents

Foreword

*T*he call to walk as sons and daughters of God, as Christ-followers, as representatives of our Heavenly Father in the earth is one of the most exciting and fulfilling pursuits we can have. If we are honest, though, the ups and downs of life and the difficulties often associated with it can leave even the most faithful believer weary and confused. We often ask, where is the glory and beauty of serving God in my life? Or, why am I experiencing so many trials and heart-wrenching situations? It's in times like these that we are especially aided by "the word of testimony" from others in the body of Christ. So often, what we need is a new framework and perspective with which to view the seasons of life. That is why *Broken for a Purpose* is so valuable. In it, Michael Bacon shares insight born of God's Word, illuminated by the wisdom of Holy Spirit, and ratified by his rich personal experiences. Pulling from the treasures that God has placed in his heart over the years, Michael shares much needed perspective for each of us that will help us cooperate with, and benefit from, God's training and breaking process in our Christian walk. *Broken for a Purpose* will encourage you to grasp God's greater plan and purpose across the seasons of life, resulting in a "glory to glory" growth and intimacy with Father God through Jesus Christ.

Chris Ellis, October 2018

Dedication

This book is dedicated to my lovely wife, Lyn Bacon, and our eight children along with our beautiful grand children. My desire is that in future years my family members will read this book and know how deeply I loved God and how critical He is to our lives. Some of them have not given their lives to Christ. I pray continually for every member of my household to be saved. I also dedicate this book to all those that have stood by me in my times of breaking. My greatest dedication is to God. I want to thank God for His endless mercy and love concerning me. Without God I would have nothing. It is because of Him that I can live in peace. He has been loving, patient and kind to me even in times where I struggled. Because of God all things are possible in my life. My love and affection for God only grows stronger as I get older.

Introduction

*B*rothers and Sisters in Christ, I pray this book is so life changing that you will not only read it, but you will feel compelled by Holy Spirit to share it with others. I believe that Holy Spirit is calling many of us into the place of brokenness so that we can be used in a greater way for the purposes of God. Let me say up front that not everyone likes the words broke, broken or brokenness. To many, these words imply that there is something wrong with them. That they are abnormal, defective or somehow incomplete. In the Kingdom of God, brokenness is a good thing. It is part of God's process to transform us into His image. To be broken means that we are made complete through the working of the Holy Spirit. When I am weak He is strong. God uses seasons of brokenness to strip out of us those things that are not like Him. Affliction, trials and tests are often part of the breaking process and are the means by which God teaches us to walk by faith and not by the flesh. Seasons of brokenness often produce the most growth in our lives. Without these seasons, many of us would not be where we are today in our relationships with God.

For me, personally, God has been taking me through the breaking process the last several years, and it has not been easy. The breaking process is critical to every believer's walk with Jesus. We cannot become who we are called to be in God without the breaking of our flesh, our mind, our emotions. There is continuous warfare between our flesh and our spirit man. The Bible teaches us that we are a new creation in Christ, but the old man will try to come back on us if we let it.

2 Corinthians 5:17
Therefore if any man be in Christ, he is a new creature: old things are passed away; behold, all things are become new.

Isaiah 43:18
Do not call to mind the former things; pay no attention to things of old.

I don't see or hear a lot of teaching on the breaking process. It doesn't seem to be a very popular topic, or we would see more teaching on the subject. Job was a man who went through more hardship than most of us would want to endure. I don't know of many people that want to willingly sign up to have a Job-like experience. It's one thing to read about one; another entirely to live or experience one. Just a few of the things Job experienced would be devastating to most of us. For example, he lost children, possessions, finances, friends, and even experienced some very painful infirmities. I am not suggesting that every person should have to have a Job-like experience, but at a minimum we must be willing to be broken. We must lay our entire life down for Christ no matter what it may cost us. It is a choice we have to make. Will we serve God at all cost, no matter the price that is required or will we resist the inner working that could change our lives for the better? Every believer has to make a choice as to whether they will submit themselves to the breaking process or not.

I believe most Christians want to serve God but are hesitant or unwilling to submit to the breaking process. Most of us are unwilling to allow God to do a complete work in our lives. We will make excuses, run from the call, or even interfere with the discipline of the Lord. Sure, we will allow God to do a little work here and there; but, when it becomes too painful, we don't want God to go any further. It's kind of like going to the dentist and getting a root canal. The pain in your tooth caused you to go to the dentist, but once the dentist begins to drill and hits a nerve, you want to jump out of the chair and run out of the dentist office. You know your only option is to either complete the surgery or live with the pain. In reality, if you don't treat the root cause, you could end up with a bad infection or, even worse, lose your tooth. We can sometimes prolong the inevitable. It's better to submit to God now, than to deal with the consequences later.

As Christians, we need major surgery and only God is qualified to do it. However, we must be willing to submit to the process. The truth is that the breaking process is very hard for most of us to endure. It is often accompanied by major attacks, setbacks, tests, and trials in our lives that can last days, months, or even years. I know for myself, I've often asked God why my breaking process has to take so long and to be so painful. At times it seems unbearable to me. Jesus continues to assure me that it is for my good and that in time I will have a full understanding of the purpose of these seasons of my life. For myself, I have purposed in my heart to fully trust and obey God no matter the cost. Each believer has to make a similar choice to experience the fullness of God in their life.

I want to be fully transparent in this book. In doing so, I will be sharing some things that are humbling and not necessarily pretty. As Christians, we all more than likely have baggage before and after we got saved that would surprise others. If people knew certain things about us, they may not see us as qualified to be in ministry or to even to be a child of God. Many of us have internal battles with our flesh and mind that we never share with anyone else. Some of us battle shame, guilt, and unworthiness because of what is in our heart and minds. For some, it is too painful or even too embarrassing to deal with. Others learn to cope with the parts of themselves that are not like Christ. There are many people that are never victorious over these areas of their lives. Many even take these undealt with areas of their lives with them to the grave, with no one ever knowing what they truly battled. If only they had allowed God to take them through the breaking process, they could have been fully healed and experienced a more victorious life in Christ. There will be some that realize too late that they could have been used by God in a greater way in their life if only they had been fully committed to being broken.

There are also some things about us that are displeasing to God – things that we overlook or underplay the importance of. If we don't cooperate with the breaking process, then these things cannot and will not be removed from our lives. As for myself, I know I am called by God to ministry, but sometimes I don't really want to pay the cost. I don't like to have to deal with or face the ugly things that are in me, especially things in my heart. You will not hear many believers admit that they battle things in their lives. Often, Christians falsely portray themselves as being perfect so that people will not see what they really struggle with or the areas where they need freedom. There is a perception that somehow Christians are perfect, but this is a lie straight from hell itself. Christians can teach people more through transparency of their weaknesses and how they overcome them, than false perfection.

Even Christian leaders struggle with areas of their lives and need God to break them. No one is exempt from the breaking process. The reality is that I am a mere man; I know that, if it weren't for God, I would be completely unworthy of the Call. I am totally dependent on God to serve Him. Without His help, and my willingness to be broken, I would be one of the worst sinners you would ever meet. Thank God for the grace He gives us. He knows our hearts, our minds, and even the hidden things we have ignored. He loves us and wants to do a redemptive work in our lives. We just need to surrender ourselves to the inner working of the Holy Spirit.

The Lord began doing a major breaking in me about two years ago. To be honest, it felt like the longest two years of my life. I felt like God literally trapped me, so I had no options available to me other than Him. In the natural, I knew God was all I needed, but, in my flesh, I didn't like having to depend on God for everything. I know that sounds crazy to the average person, but think about it. As an example, you are used to being able to work and make money, but now God won't allow you to work and has blocked every attempt to get a job. Imagine how you would feel during this time of your life. This was a very difficult time in my life. A little background leading up to this period. I have two master's degrees and am almost done with my doctorate degree; yet during this season, no man would give me a job, even an entry-level job. It all began with a job layoff, followed by the Lord giving me the following scripture verse. Matthew 16:25 reads: *"For whosoever will save his life shall lose it: and whosoever will lose his life for my sake shall find it."* I had no understanding of this verse until I went through my breaking season. I did not realize that my life is not my own. Yes, I knew that was what the Bible teaches, but it was not a revelation to me personally. About a year into the layoff I was getting desperate for a job, because I had a lot of bills pilling up. It was during that time that I was offered a great job working with a Christian company that offered an attractive relocation package, large salary, five weeks of vacation per year, and near the beach. It was a dream job scenario. I initially took the job offer, but then I heard the Lord remind me of what He said in Matthew 16:25. He spoke these words to me, "Michael, did I tell you to take that job?" I knew as soon as I heard the question, that I had made a mistake. I had taken the job without even consulting the Lord. I was so tired of the breaking season I was in that I was trying to find an early exit. Only God wasn't finished breaking me during this time, so I had to obey Him and turn the job down.

Part of brokenness is doing what God says even if it doesn't make sense at the time. I am sure God had a reason for this. Maybe it was a test of my obedience or maybe it wasn't the right job for me. I don't know, but I had to obey God so that I didn't have to go through the breaking process all over again. The hard part about this job offer was that I would have had to close down our church and leave the ministry God had called us to. My decision to take this job would not only affect me, but all those that were in our church. Sometimes things are bigger than we are and we must trust God for the decisions He makes on our behalf. As I sit here and write this book, I have no regrets in trusting God.

God has a way of cornering us. He has a way of challenging us to make Him Lord in every area of our life. He desires only the best for us. However, as He has shown me, we must be broken before we are usable in the Kingdom of God. One of the best analogies Jesus gave me about brokenness is that of a wild stallion (horse). Most of us are wild in nature. Our flesh is wild in that it does what it feels led to do when it feels led to do it. We often follow the desires of our flesh more than we do the leading of the Holy Spirit. The Lord showed me that every Christian starts out as a wild horse. Our flesh is rebellious in nature. It is wild and unruly. In order for our lives to be usable by God, we have to be broken like that horse so that we can be trusted to carry men safely.

Many of you reading this introduction will begin to feel the Holy Spirit move on you. God is calling many of us into a corral where we are no longer in control of our lives. We must choose to submit to the breaking process so we will be usable by God. Many of us want God to use us, but it all begins with submitting to the breaking process. The benefits of the breaking process are beyond human understanding. The Lord has shown me that we look at brokenness the wrong way. I used to think of brokenness as the end of someone's dreams. A person stripped of their dignity and well being. I viewed it by what they lost or used to have. What the Lord has shown me is that brokenness is a beautiful thing because through it, we are being transformed from the old man into a new creation. All things have now become new. 2 Corinthians 5:17 says, "Therefore if any man *be* in Christ, *he is* a new creature: old things are passed away; behold, all things are become new." Even our mind changes, and how we see things will also change. Brokenness is truly the key to every believer's freedom.

CHAPTER 1

The Difference Between Horses and Donkeys

When I was a child, I was fascinated by horses. My aunt and her friend had a few horses that they kept at my grandparents' house in upstate New York. During the summers, I would go up there and watch the horses as they ran around the fenced pasture. They were so beautiful to look at, and I would watch them for hours. I was mesmerized by their beauty and strength. I loved to see them shake their manes and hear the loud snorting sounds they made. Yet, I was also somewhat terrified of them. Whenever I tried to feed them an apple or some vegetable leaves, they would show me their teeth. A few times I thought they were going to bite my hand off! I learned to put the food in the palm of my hand for them to feed. At times the horses were also temperamental and would charge at you if you tried to come near them, especially if they were not familiar with you. The most terrifying time for me was when I went for my first horseback ride. One day my aunt put me up on the horse and walked us down a dirt road. She played a joke on me and told me to make a clicking sound with my mouth. Not knowing anything about horses, I went along with it. As soon as I did, the horse went into a full trot. Needless to say, it really terrified me. I cried and cried and never wanted to go on that horse again. I was around ten years old or younger, and I will never forget it. To this day, I cannot imagine what would have happened if that horse had not been domesticated and trained. The trotting was enough to scare me, but what if I had been on an undisciplined and unruly horse? Would it have run wildly out of control or tried to buck me off? Without the right training that horse could have seriously hurt me. Thankfully, this horse was trained and disciplined.

Horses are incredible creatures, but it also takes a skilled person to train and ride a horse. Horses cannot be handled or ridden by men unless they have gone through a breaking and have been trained and prepared to be of service.

Proverbs 21:31
The horse is prepared against the day of battle: but safety is of the LORD.

When I first read this Bible verse, I got a picture in my head of a large powerful horse that would take its master into battle. I envisioned a muscular body with legs that would give the horse incredible speed. I also imagined it to be a horse that is fully disciplined and obeys its master. It is a horse that has no fear of people, weapons, or loud booming sounds of war. It is a horse that would charge in the face of the enemy. It is a horse that is not only trained, but fully prepared for battle.

The Lord showed me that this is very similar to what He is doing with the church today. We are being prepared as an army of God to rule and reign with Him forever and ever.

Revelation 19:11-16

And I saw heaven opened, and behold a white horse; and he that sat upon him was called Faithful and True, and in righteousness he doth judge and make war.

His eyes were as a flame of fire, and on his head were many crowns; and he had a name written, that no man knew, but he himself.

And he was clothed with a vesture dipped in blood: and his name is called The Word of God.

And the armies which were in heaven followed him upon white horses, clothed in fine linen, white and clean.

And out of his mouth goeth a sharp sword, that with it he should smite the nations: and he shall rule them with a rod of iron: and he treadeth the winepress of the fierceness and wrath of Almighty God.

And he hath on his vesture and on his thigh a name written, KING OF KINGS, AND LORD OF LORDS.

When Christ returns, He is not returning alone, but He will be riding on a horse. He is not coming on just any horse, but a white horse. God spoke to me and said that the horse represents His church. The Bible says that He will return for a church without spot or blemish. The

3

horse is white because it has been purified and made clean by the blood of Jesus. It is a church that has been tried, tested, and proven true. It is a church that has been broken of anything that is not Christ like. It's a church that is broken and proven to be obedient to Christ. It's a church that has been cleansed of all sin, all disobedience, and all stubbornness of the flesh.

Ephesians 5:27
That he might present it to himself a glorious church, not having spot, or wrinkle, or any such thing; but that it should be holy and without blemish.

When Jesus was on earth the first time, He walked in complete humility. Instead of assuming His Kingly position, He allowed men and Satan to persecute, beat, whip, and hang Him on a cross. He never once tried to defend Himself. He could have ruled and reigned on earth; however, instead, walked as a humble and broken servant. His mind, His will, His emotions, and even His body were fully committed to God. He displayed that humility again when He rode a donkey into town instead of a horse. As we read in Revelations 19:11, when He returns for His church, He will be coming as King of Kings and Lord of Lords – He will be riding on a horse, not a donkey. This represents the outcome of brokenness. Jesus allowed God to break Him. He allowed God to complete the work He was doing in His life. He was demonstrating the process of dealing with our mind, body and emotions. Jesus was showing the church that even He had to go through seasons of humility and brokenness before He was ready to fulfill

His will and destiny on this earth. We should learn from Jesus's example.

Matthew 21:7
And brought the ass, and the colt, and put on them their clothes, and they set him thereon.

As Christians, we are following the same footsteps of Jesus. We must humble ourselves like Christ did. We must allow God to break us, so we can be who God has called us to be. We must be changed from our old man to the new creation He intended us to be.

Keeping with the analogy of the horse, God must remove all stubbornness from our lives. We are being transformed from a donkey to a horse. Mankind in its natural state is equivalent to a mule or a hinny. A mule is the offspring of a male donkey and female horse that have mated. A hinny is produced when you breed a stallion or male horse with a female donkey. Mules, as an example, possess characteristics of both of their parents, but are typically sterile and cannot reproduce. Other than one known case, hinnies also cannot reproduce. Jesus wants to reproduce Himself in us, but for that to happen He has to remove any stubbornness and rebellion that may exist in our lives. He must remove all works of the flesh so that only His characteristics remain within us. We cannot have the characteristics of a donkey and a horse at the same time. Just as we cannot have characteristic of the flesh and the spirit competing against each other. The spirit must rule over the flesh. This only happens through brokenness.

Galatians 5:17
For the flesh lusteth against the Spirit, and the Spirit against the flesh: and these are contrary the one to the other: so that ye cannot do the things that ye would.

As believers we often demonstrate characteristics that are similar to a donkey. Below I will give some of the characteristics that donkeys have that are common to mankind and the flesh.

Characteristics of Donkeys and How They Compare to Men:

- Have a very good memory that can last up to 25 years
  - Remembering the former things
  - Not moving forward in what God has for them
- Are very stubborn
  - Their flesh is strong and hard to break
  - They tend to refuse to obey
- Are very independent in their thinking
  - They don't take counsel and ignore wisdom
  - They don't listen to their masters and walk in disobedience
- Can hear other donkeys up to 60 miles away
  - They listen to what others say instead of what God says
  - Always listening in on everyone else's business
- Will not do anything they think is unsafe
  - Will not walk by faith but rely on what their eyes or what circumstances suggest

- Are a servant animal that is used for hard labor
  - Works of the flesh versus being led by the spirit

As we allow God to break us and make us more like Him, our character changes from donkey like characteristics to the characteristics of horses.

Characteristics of Horses and How They Compare to the Word:

- Flees to defend itself against predators
  - The Bible says to flee from Satan or Sin
- Prefers to roam in herds for protection
  - The Bible says to not forsake the assembling of ourselves together as is the manner of some
- A very social animal that values friendships
  - Prefer others over yourselves
  - Love one another like Christ loves the church
- Creature of habit
  - We are to be disciplined and walk in obedience
- A need for constant movement
  - God is always on the move
  - When God moves we move with Him

Ecclesiastes 3:18-21
I said in mine heart concerning the estate of the sons of men, that God might manifest them, and that they might see that they themselves are beasts.

For that which befalleth the sons of men befalleth beasts; even one thing befalleth them: as the one dieth, so dieth the other; yea, they have all one breath; so that a man hath no preeminence above a beast: for all is vanity.

All go unto one place; all are of the dust, and all turn to dust again.

Who knoweth the spirit of man that goeth upward, and the spirit of the beast that goeth downward to the earth?

The Bible says that man is no different than a beast or an animal. Men are similar to a mix or cross-breed between a donkey and a horse. We have some characteristics of the flesh and some characteristics of the spirit. Our walk with God is a process, whereby God is removing those things that are of the flesh so that the spirit can live within us. The Bible says in 2 Corinthians 3:18 *"But we all, with open face beholding as in a glass the glory of the Lord, are changed into the same image from glory to glory, even as by the Spirit of the Lord."* See, there is a process by which we are being made into His image. We are being taken from being a stubborn donkey to being a horse that is fit for Jesus to ride upon. God is removing all the characteristics of the donkey that are holding us back from being part of the Kingdom of God. This is what I refer to as the Breaking Process. Each of us needs to be broken for God to be able to ride on us or to use us in His Kingdom.

CHAPTER 2

The Breaking Process and How it Works

We can learn a lot about the breaking process from how cowboys and trainers break-in horses. A horse must be transformed from a wild beast to a usable vessel. The breaking process is necessary or the horse would be unpredictable and unable to be trusted with human lives. There are countless stories about horses with bad temperaments – not having been fully trained or trained properly – that have bucked people off of them, charged at someone, or hooved a person to death. While horses are nice to look at, they can be very mean and temperamental in nature. In particular, stallions, like donkeys, can be very stubborn animals. The breaking of a stallion is critical and is the foundation that all other healthy and trained behaviors are built upon. Horses have to be taken through a process to prepare them for service to their owners. Each horse has a function that the owner has in mind. Training may vary, depending on the service the horse will have to perform. For example, there are rider horses that carry people, and there are labor horses that are used for plowing fields. There are also wagon horses that pull carriages, and war horses are used for war. Lastly, there are pet horses that are domesticated and are gentle with people.

Steps of the Breaking Process

Step 1: Capturing the Horse

First, the horse has to be taken from its natural habitat. It cannot be left to go and do as it pleases. The stallion is very territorial and domineering in nature. It believes it is in charge of all the other horses and will fight to protect the herd and its position as lead stallion. It is wild in nature. It is not under anyone's authority or control. It is very independent and intelligent, so it is also hard to catch. While most horses will flee from their enemies, stallions will stay to fight and even attack their predators.

Horses are very powerful animals that can run at very high speeds, which make them difficult to catch by men. The person capturing the horse must be very smart and have experience with horses in order to successfully catch one. Like we see in the movies, most of the time cowboys use lassos to catch the horse so that it cannot run away. Many times the horse will put up a fight once the lasso is placed around their neck. Initially the horse will try to pull away or buck, and sometimes use their legs to try to run or fight if necessary. Eventually, the horse wears out and the cowboy is able to take it into captivity. After a horse is captured it is placed in a corral to await training. Some horses are very irritable and anxious once they are corralled.

Their nature is to roam freely to do as they please, but now they are under someone else's power and control versus their own. They may act nervous, fearful, or anxious until they get used to their new environment and limitations.

Isaiah 28:13
But the word of the Lord was unto them precept upon precept, precept upon precept; line upon line, line upon line; here a little, and there a little; that they might go, and fall backward, and be broken, and snared, and taken.

This is an interesting verse because it shows that the Lord sometimes allows us to fall backward or be broken as part of the process to snare or capture us in order to fulfill His purpose in our life. When we are facing difficult situations or being broken, we often get anxious, fearful, or worried about what is happening. Most people dislike attacks, trials, or setbacks in their lives. It is human nature to want everything to go well with us. People are creatures of habit and many don't like any kind of change (good or bad). I used to view setbacks as bothersome, until one-day Holy Spirit taught me that setbacks sometimes are part of God's plan to slow us down long enough for God to capture us, so He can break us. We have to be captured and surrender to God before He can work with us and break us. If we are still in control of our lives and doing as we please, then it is impossible for God to do a work in us. We must die to ourselves and surrender to God fully in all areas of our lives.

Step 2: Breaking the Horse

A horse must be broken, or it will not be a suitable vessel to be used by men. If the horse is not broken, then it cannot be ridden or trusted with the responsibility of carrying people. An unbroken horse is highly unpredictable and even dangerous to people. If the horse is strong-willed, the breaking can take a long time; however, some horses are more cooperative than others.

Just like humans, there are some really stubborn and rebellious horses. The breaking is never an easy process. You are dealing with a horse's will and emotions. Some horses deal with anxiety, stress, and fear. Breaking the horse means dealing with their temperament and old ways, to get it to conform to a new behavior. There are different ways to break a horse. Depending on the horse the process may vary.

Step 3: Training the horse

It is not enough to break a horse. Depending on how the horse is going to be used, there is additional training that has to happen. Horses who have been broken have been taught to submit to their master, but they have not necessarily been taught what is necessary to be used properly. As I mentioned earlier, some horses will be used to carry loads, or perhaps to carry people. Rider horses have to be taught to carry weight of a person. They also have to submit to wearing a saddle and bridle. They are taught by use of bridle, reins, and spurs. Each of these is an instrument used to be lead or guide the horse in the right direction or to obedience. The bridle and reins are used to show the horse what direction they need to go. They are also used to stop the horse when needed. The spurs are used to direct a horse to go forward or in a direction. They can be used to increase speed as well. The horse learns that when a rider uses a particular instrument there is a corresponding command. The rider also uses voice commands to tell the horse what to do. There are several things the horse has to learn in order to be fit for service. This process often takes time and patience.

The master or trainer must have a great deal of patience in order to effectively train the horse. If a horse is treated harshly or forced through rough-riding, then the horse will later become unpredictable in terms of behavior. Rough riding is a process where the trainer does not take the time to earn the trust of the horse. Instead, they use harsh techniques to make the horse submit quickly to being ridden. While the trainer may be able to initially ride the horse, it can also introduce behavioral problems in the long run because trust has not been established. The best training is one that teaches the horse to comply or being obedient without having to mistreat it. The horse will more naturally comply with the breaking process in this case.

Step 4: Testing the horse

The temperament of your horse is critical to understand. Even after the breaking and training, you still need to test the horse to ensure it has the right temperament for the role for which it will be used. Consider how the horse was broken and the behaviors the horse has exhibited during the process. In our lives, testing is also a huge part of the breaking process. God will often allow us to go through something and then later allow us to be tested in that area to see how we will respond this time versus before the breaking occurred in our lives. If we pass the test, then God knows we are ready to be used in that area.

In the natural horses are tested by their trainers. If a horse is to be considered as a harness horse it must have the right temperament. One way that trainers will test horses is to make sudden sounds or disturbances to see how they react. If the horse starts bolting or panicking, then the trainer knows this horse is not fit for service.

Testing your horse is similar to how God tests man. He is always testing us to see if we will walk in the spirit or by the flesh. How we react to situations shows whether we are growing in God's word or if there is yet more breaking or training that needs to take place. Most people hate tests, but the outcomes of tests show us whether we're ready or need more training. Like horses, we need to be broken and then prepared for use in the Kingdom of God.

CHAPTER 3

Horse Breaking

A horse that is trained to be ridden or that pulls a wagon is called **broke**. Most horse lovers don't like the word broke or broken because it implies that the training was done by force against the horse's will in order to break its spirit down. It is a very uncompassionate way to train a horse. As we see in western movies, horses were rounded up off the range. Cowboys used a method called "bucked out" to teach a horse to be ridden. With this technique, the cowboy would jump on the horse and ride it until it stopped bucking against the rider. This would often be a violent process as the horse would fight like crazy to get the rider off of it's back. The cowboy would then pull tightly on the reins until the horse lost its will to fight. In many cases, the cowboy would even beat or whip the horse into compliance. While the horse may eventually comply and be of immediate use, it may later develop rebellious behaviors or develop bad temperaments that would make them unreliable or unpredictable to riders. Imagine if God did this to us. Thankfully, God takes a more loving and patient approach with us. Horse trainers typically

15

use a softer approach to training horses which is called "gentle breaking." This training does require more patience from the trainer and may take a lot longer, but in the end produces better results. Afterwards, these horses are considered to be "well broke", which means that they are well trained and understand the commands given them. Often, horses that receive this type of training have a gentler spirit, and are more obedient than horses who have been rough ridden.

One of the things that is interesting about horse-breaking is that there are different types of breaking-in that have to happen, depending on what type of work the horse will do. Saddle-breaking is training a horse to carry a rider. Harness-breaking is training a horse to pull a vehicle. Depending on the purpose, the training and the breaking process is different. Some training takes longer and is more difficult than other training. Also, not every horse has the right temperament to reliably pull a wagon. Some horses don't have the strength or endurance to carry loads. They may be good at carrying a rider, but they don't have the ability to pull a wagon or a vehicle. Some horses spook too easily and would not be reliable enough to be trusted with pulling a wagon or people.

Unfortunately, we have some trainers that get impatient and will not follow the proper steps to training. Some trainers get in a rush, and don't take time to get to know their horse to understand their temperament or earn their trust. Some trainers will take a rider horse and connect it to a carriage and expect the horse to automatically pull it down the street. Without taking the correct training steps, the horse may run from the carriage, because it fears it. The horse actually thinks the carriage is chasing it. In many cases this ends up resulting in injury or a crash. When this happens the horse then loses its trust and confidence and may not be a good candidate to carry loads or people from that time forth. Depending on the use of the horse, it must meet certain qualifications. Mostly, behavioral qualifications. Horses that are overly aggressive can chase animals, or bite people. Some may even refuse to comply to basic commands. The person driving a carriage must be able to trust the horse to obey at all times.

There are also what we call war horses. War horses have to be trained for strength, speed, and obedience. They cannot be stubborn, independent, unruly, or temperamental. In a wartime situation, they will be exposed to the weather elements, and oncoming attacks from the enemy. War horses cannot be easily spooked by loud noises as an example. Proper training must be provided before wartime situations so that they can overcome their fears and be obedient to their masters. They cannot be fearful of guns, bullets or even explosions. This type of horse has to be fully disciplined and have the right personality to be useful to the rider. Now, let's take this analogy of breaking horses and apply it to those called by God to do His will and purpose on this earth.

Each of us is in this earth (pasture) grazing and loving life. We are a free stallion, running around and doing as we please in the world. Then, we are chosen by God. He gathers us from the pasture. He puts His brand on us (His mark) so that everyone knows we belong to Him. We are no longer wandering and doing what we want to do. We are now being broken (trained). Initially, everyone is selected to be a rider horse. We are to point people to Jesus. Everyone goes through the process of becoming a new creature in Christ. We are being transformed into His image. That process begins with us dying to ourselves, our agendas, our ways.

Galatians 2:20
I have been crucified with Christ; and it is no longer I who live, but Christ lives in me; and the life which I now live in the flesh I live by faith in the Son of God, who loved me and gave Himself up for me.

John 3:30
He must increase, but I must decrease.

What we are dying to is that old man. The rebellious stallion that we used to be is now being transformed and conformed into God's image. Except, God does not rough-ride us. He patiently and lovingly breaks us and molds us into His image from one level of glory to another level of glory. He is a kind and merciful God that only has the best in mind for each of us.

2 Corinthians 3:18
But we all, with open face beholding as in a glass the glory of the Lord, are changed into the same image from glory to glory, even as by the Spirit of the Lord.

Thankfully, God has such a love for His servants that He breaks them, so they can be usable for His kingdom. I believe that God looks at our hearts to see how broken we have become. Brokenness is not just on the outside, it's also on the inside. It is the issues of the heart that God cares most about. God is always searching our hearts to see if they are fully surrendered to Him. I will also note that, if you are called to a specific ministry or office, you may have to also go through additional breaking compared to the average believer; because you are called to carry the load of many people, like a harness horse. This doesn't imply that anyone is excused from being broken, because every believer is required go through this process regardless of our call or purpose. However, God will use those that are most willing to be broken to do His will and fulfill His purpose. Without being broken, we are unable to be used by God to the level that He desires us to be used. He cannot trust us to be fit for service if we are unwilling to yield our minds, our hearts and lives unto Him. As Christians, it is not just our lives that are affected by our undealt with issues. If we don't allow God to break us, we affect everyone we come in contact with.

The responsibilities given to us as believers can be overwhelming at times. You must be broken so that you will reflect the Father's love for others. If you are called to an apostolic or pastoral ministry, you can expect to go through rejection, disappointment, delays, financial issues, and even defamation. You cannot be an effective believer or leader when you have hidden heart issues such as anger, unforgiveness, a critical spirit, a judgmental spirit, a man-pleasing spirit, or fear. You are responsible not only for your safety but the safety of God's people and all that He has entrusted you with. There is much more at stake when you are a harness horse than a rider horse. A harness horse can kill many people if not fully broken and trained versus a rider horse that may kill a single rider it carries on its back. All believers need to submit to being broken, but ministry leaders are held to even a higher standard.

Many of you are being broken to be a harness horse. It is not an easy process, and there are times when the weight of things will seem unbearable. It will feel like your flesh is dying and God is requiring more and more out of you. Things will feel like they are closing in around you. The pastures are right there, but you can't run freely in them anymore. You used to be able to do what you wanted to do, when you wanted to, but now you are only able to move when God says to move. You are God's servant, and you have to lay down your life to serve Him no matter what the cost is to you. It may very well cost you everything in order to be fully broken and usable to God. It is part of the process of becoming an instrument God can truly use.

Think and meditate on this scripture for a moment.

Matthew 16:25
For whosoever will save his life shall lose it: and whosoever will lose his life for my sake shall find it.

We can choose to fully submit or not fully submit to the breaking process. It's our choice, and God has given us a free will to choose who we will serve. His desire is that each of us will freely submit to the "gentle breaking" versus us having to go through the "rough breaking."

Jonah was a prophet who decided he didn't like what God was asking him to do, so he decided to run from God. Many people are running from God in this hour. God will let you run for a while, but, in the end, He will require that you fully submit to His will in your life. In the case of Jonah, God sent a fish to swallow him up, and then, after he broke him in the belly of that whale, God had the fish take him back where he was told to go. Many believe that this fish was actually a whale.

It's very interesting about what happens when you are swallowed by a whale. There are documented cases on the internet of men who were swallowed by a whale and lived to talk about it. In one case, a man named James Bartley was on a whaling expedition when his boat was attacked by a large whale and was swallowed whole in the process. Other whalers on the expedition did not realize that the whale had swallowed him and later killed the whale. They did not find out until later after they had skinned the whale that Bartley was inside. It turns out that he had been in the whale for over 36 hours. By this time the gastric juices of the whale's belly had bleached his skin, and he was blind the rest of his life.

God showed me that, in his rebellion, Jonah had to be imprisoned or removed from his old life. Then the breaking and cleansing process happened. He was being made white or clean by the gastric juices that attacked his flesh. Just like the white horse Jesus will one day ride upon, we too will be purified. Lastly, he lost his ability to see like his old man saw. Now he was completely dependent on God to take him where he should go.

John 21:18
Verily, verily, I say unto thee, When thou wast young, thou girdedst thyself, and walkedst whither thou wouldest: but when thou shalt be old, thou shalt stretch forth thy hands, and another shall gird thee, and carry thee whither thou wouldest not.

God is preparing each believer for greater works and greater things in Him. In order for these greater works to happen, God has to first break each of us so that the works of the flesh are destroyed. If the flesh is not dealt with, then it is impossible to walk in the Spirit and accomplish the will and purpose of God. God takes us as His own, breaks us from the old ways, and we become a new creation in Christ, Jesus. The more we cooperate with the breaking process, the more likely we are to be usable by God. Truly, there are many evil spirits trying to influence man in this hour. God is looking for a remnant people that He can trust to do His will on earth. Are you willing for God to use you to the point where it is no longer you, but Christ living through you? That is a question all of us must answer for ourselves.

CHAPTER 4

What is God Breaking in Us?

*M*any of us don't recognize or understand why God would want to break us. In fact, I don't think many people are even open to the idea of being broken. The reality is that many of us are not where God wants us to be, spiritually speaking. God created us with a particular purpose; yet to a large degree, mankind is far from what He intended. God breaks us, because He sees things in us that are not like Him. His will for us is that we are less and less like us, and more and more like Him. We were, in fact, created to be like God.

Genesis 1:26-28
And God said, Let us make man in our image, after our likeness: and let them have dominion over the fish of the sea, and over the fowl of the air, and over the cattle, and over all the earth, and over every creeping thing that creepeth upon the earth.

The first thing this verse tells us is that we were made in "our image." This passage has always intrigued me, because I always thought it would or should say that we were made in the image of God. This verse shows us that in the very beginning of time that the Trinity (Father, Son, Holy Spirit) existed. The Trinity is three distinct persons in one. Mankind was made in the image of the Father, the Son, and the Holy Spirit. Mankind is multi-dimensional, in that we were meant to have characteristics of all three persons not just one. This is so important, because the qualities we get from each person are unique to that person yet compliment or complete the other person. Jesus tells His disciples that it was necessary that He die so that He could send to us the Holy Spirit who was to be our helper, teacher, and our comforter.

It is important to understand that we were designed a particular way. The other thing that we notice in Genesis is that mankind was created to walk in dominion. We were never supposed to be defeated or a victim to sin or the ways of this world. We were put here to rule over and subdue the world, yet most Christians are victims instead of rulers. Part of what God is doing is to break us to the point where He can remove anything that is interfering with our ability to rule and reign with Him. It is possible, Church, to come to a place of growth where we are doing greater things than Jesus did when He was on the earth. In fact, Jesus says in John 14:12 that "*We will do greater things than these, because He was going to the Father.*"

His departure from this earth made it possible for us to walk in the fullness of what God intended for us. God has begun a good work in the lives of those that are willing to be broken. As part of that good work, God looks inside each of us and identifies that which is in us that is stopping us from doing great things in His name. For each person, God is breaking us of something that is specific to our lives. Some of the areas God deals with are sin, lust of the flesh, love of money, pride, fear, anger, laziness, unforgiveness, false doctrines, unbelief, fear of man, and a man pleasing spirit.

Sin

Sin is anything that separates us from the presence of God. It is anything in us that is not like God. The result of sin in our lives is broken fellowship with God. We cannot have a relationship with God and continue to sin. The Lord takes us through the process of dealing with any area of our lives that is not like Him. He will deal with the issues of our hearts, our attitudes, our mindsets, the lust of our flesh, idolatry, areas of defilement, and any disobedience that may be in our lives. As God breaks us, He creates within us a repentant heart so that we will be freed from all areas of sin. If we humble ourselves and confess and renounce areas of sin in our lives, then fellowship and blessings will be restored. It is God's intention that we are continually growing in the Lord. He is looking for sons and daughters who are maturing and giving more and more of their lives to God. We cannot choose to be disobedient and expect to know God intimately. Jesus gave His life so that we could be free of sin and any consequences of sin. He will allow us to be broken as part of the process of removing sinful areas of our lives. I, for one, would rather be broken here on earth than to have to one day give an account for my disobedience.

25

The Bible says in 1 John 1:9 that *"If we confess our sins, then He is able to forgive us our sins and to cleanse us from all righteousness."* Sometimes, we are blind to our sins. We have unknown sins, or we have not truly seen ourselves like God has seen us. So God allows us to be broken so that we can clearly see the areas that we are falling short in and repent. Truthfully, when things are going well, most people don't take the time to ask God where they have sinned and fallen short; but, when things go bad, most people will cry out to Him and seek Him. I believe God is showing His love and mercy when He allows us to be broken or tested. The Bible says in Hebrews 12:6 that *"He disciplines those that He loves."* Consider it an honor when God deals with the sins in your life. He has considered you worthy to be changed into His image.

Lust of the Flesh

The lust of the flesh is one of the toughest areas God has to deal with in most Christians, especially with the increase of carnality and sexual perversion we see in in the United States of America. Hollywood and society are openly promoting sexual perversion through signs, billboards, media, television, movies, and music. The eyes are the gateway to the soul. Everywhere you look you will find sex, pornography, and lewdness. There is no longer a moral filter that society lives by to protect those that don't want to be exposed to such things. In fact, Hollywood and even our government is being very aggressive in its perversion of man's sexuality and is openly promoting homosexual and transgender lifestyles. The lust of the flesh is a huge issue in the church, too. Many Christians are secretly living ungodly sensual lifestyles and, yet, also trying to serve God. The Bible talks about the dangers of fornication, adultery, and homosexuality.

1 Corinthians 6:9
Know ye not that the unrighteous shall not inherit the kingdom of God? Be not deceived: neither fornicators, nor idolaters, nor adulterers, nor effeminate, nor abusers of themselves with mankind.

I have traveled internationally and I have to say that sexual perversion and related demonic spirits are most strong in the United States and Europe. I have seen those spirits in operation mostly in these areas. Not to say that these spirits are not in operation elsewhere, but it seems that there are major strongholds in the United States and throughout Europe. Oddly, these are the areas where Christianity is supposed to have more influence. (Although, in the United Kingdom I have witnessed a major falling away from the faith and fear that the United States is right behind it.) Sexual immorality may very well be the reason for many leaving their faith. God is breaking the remnant people that are willing to be broken for His sake, so He can remove these types of spirits and assignments. We cannot fornicate with the world and be effective for the Kingdom of God. We must repent of these lifestyles. Some people are so in love with sex that they have made sex their god. It has become a form of idolatry in our nation. It is a god unto itself. The Bible teaches us that we serve a jealous God and He will not allow us to serve or worship other gods. If you are struggling with sex or sexual immorality of any kind, pray and ask God to deliver you in these areas so that you can be restored to fellowship with God.

Love of Money

Many of us have lost sight of what is important in life. We were not created to make money. For many Americans, our sole purpose every day is waking up and making more money. We can become obsessed over making money and more money. The love of money is a very bad thing, because those that love money more than God have made it their god. Yes, money is many Americans' god. It is not that money itself is bad or evil. In fact, money can be a great tool if used correctly to advance the kingdom of God. However, the love of money is a bad thing.

1 Timothy 6:10
For the love of money is the root of all evil: which while some coveted after, they have erred from the faith, and pierced themselves through with many sorrows.

One of the challenges believers face is our perception of money. Money is not the answer to all our problems. God is the answer. Christians should never turn to something else over God. The Bible teaches us that God is our provider. Your employer is not your provider. Your savings account and investments will not save you in a time of disaster. Only God can care for you and your family. Without God or God's help we have nothing. No amount of money in this world can save us from our problems. Only God can save us from difficult situations. God wants His people dependent on Him not money.

God will allow us to be broken and to be tested if only to teach us to turn to Him for our needs. God wants us to depend on Him, not the things of this world. I have experienced this first hand. I had a job paying six figures a year, but God allowed me to be broken, and go jobless for almost two years. At first, I was very angry about it. I was upset with God for allowing this to happen, until I realized that God was doing this for my own good. See, I had always overworked in order to have something. I was not trusting God and allowing God to be my provider. I was doing things in my own strength. I was making my own wealth through toil and stress. The positions I held were very stressful and my health was deteriorating quickly.

God had a plan for my life and I was trying to be faithful in that call, but I was doing way too much by myself. God showed me that one of the areas He needed to deal with in me was the love of money. I was looking for money to be my answer instead of allowing God to be my answer. I am thankful for this time in my life, because I am now dependent on God for everything and I do mean everything. Yet, for those few years, I never missed a bill thanks to God. I went from a high income to practically nothing and yet God sustained my family the whole time without interruption. Everything we needed was provided, not only for us personally, but even for the church that we pastor. There were days I wondered if God would show up, but He did every time. It is better to trust God than to lean on our own strength and abilities. Ask God to show you any areas of repentance related to the love of money and get your heart right today. God is your provider. He cares for your soul. Trust Him and He will meet every need you have.

Pride

If you ask most people if they are prideful, they would most likely deny it. Most people who are prideful have a hard time seeing it in themselves. We know that the most prideful being in the universe is the devil. It was because of his pride that he rebelled against God in heaven, yet he was not content with rebelling against God by himself. He also convinced one third of the angels to rebel against God too. He didn't stop there either. He is causing a large part of humanity to rebel against God too. All of the devil is doing is tied to the spirit of pride. Satan's sin is that he aspired to take God's place. He was not content loving God or serving God. He wanted to be God.

Pride defined is "looking at yourself more highly than you should." Pride can manifest itself in different ways. It can lack humility, be selfish in nature, be self absorbed, refuse counsel of others, or not allow others to help us when we need it the most. I have seen many people who cannot receive from others because of pride. They go through a hardship and refuse to let others help. This too is a form of pride. The Bible teaches that right before a man falls he enters into pride. God has a way of allowing us to fall or to be broken to get our attention so that we can see that we have entered into pride. God wants us to be careful not to become prideful. I have seen ministers who are preaching the gospel who have become prideful. They are so blinded by pride that they cannot see that they are puffed up and arrogant. They are close to a fall but cannot see it. Satan himself had to be humbled, so God allowed him to fall out of grace from heaven down to the earth. Satan will never repent. He has way too much pride to repent. However, God wishes for every man to repent of his pride. Satan and his fallen angels were not made in the image of God, but man was made in the image of the Father, Son, and Holy Spirit. God made us to be like Him. Angels were not given this privilege, but man was given it. That is one of the reasons that Satan is after the church. He is jealous of the position God has given man in Heaven. God is contending with the devil, and he will contend with anyone that walks in pride. There is only one God, and there can only be one God. We must repent of any pride in our lives.

Anger

We see so much anger in people today. Even in the church, we see people that come for counseling and deliverance that are really struggling with anger. God says to be angry but not to sin. Uncontrolled anger can lead to sin. Part of brokenness is dealing with the root causes of anger. What is making you so angry? What events or situations trigger feelings of anger? If you are angry, why are you so angry? Is there a root issue that is causing you to be angry? When you get angry are you also sinning? Anger is a huge issue in Christians. If we don't deal with our anger it may also fester and turn into other more destructive things such as unfor-giveness, bitterness, resentment, hatred, rage, and even murder. God would rather break us than to let anger turn into something far worse. We need to be honest with

31

ourselves and clearly see what it is that is causing us to be angry and deal with it appropriately. We can ask God to show us what it is that is making us so angry. He will show you if you ask Him. He will speak to you and show you even hidden things in your heart. He will expose every root cause of anger. When we spend time with the Father, we receive His heart. If there are anger issues, they can prevent us from being close to God. He will often use brokenness as a way of showing roots of anger that need to be dealt with.

Laziness

Jesus is not coming back for a bride that is asleep. He is calling the sheep out of their slumber. Laziness is a form of wickedness. Proverbs 10:5 says, "*He that gathereth in summer is a wise son: but he that sleepeth in harvest is a son that causeth shame.*" When we are lazy or practice laziness we are lacking wisdom. James 2:14 says, "What *does it* profit, my brethren, if someone says he has faith but does not have works? Can faith save him?" Even faith requires us to do something to demonstrate that we believe. We cannot sit around and do nothing and call it faith. God will often bring brokenness so that we are forced to step out in faith. The Lord has to remove the spirit of laziness from our lives. Man was created with a purpose. Adam was put in the garden to work it and take care of it. This is discussed in Genesis 2:15. Adam and Eve's purpose was also to have fellowship with God. Many people are not spending time with the Lord or fellowshipping with Him due to a lazy spirit. For me, I had this vision of Adam and Eve sitting around the garden singing and resting all the time. That is not what God designed us to do. We have work to do church. Colossians 3:23 says, *"And whatsoever ye do, do it heartily, as to the Lord, and not unto me..."* Ecclesiastes 9:10 says, *"Whatsoever thy hand findeth to do, do it with thy might; for there is no work, nor device, nor knowledge, nor wisdom, in the grave, whither thou goest."*

It is clear that the Bible instructs us to work. We cannot be physically or spiritually lazy and expect things to work out for us. Proverbs 10:14 says, *"Lazy hands make for poverty."* We also have 1 Timothy 5:8 that says, *"But if any provide not for his own, and specially for those of his own house, he hath denied the faith, and is worse than an infidel."* There is a spirit of laziness in the corporate church. It is commonly said that 20% of the people do 80% of the work, as well as giving financially. However, there are many Christians that say that they want to be used by God to do His work. Most are not obeying God in even the most basic areas of their lives. Laziness keeps them from achieving greatness for God. Luke 16:10 says, *"He that is faithful in that which is least is faithful also in much: and he that is unjust in the least is unjust also in much."* This is a kingdom principle. People want to take short cuts to be promoted, but the first shall be last, and the last shall be first. God also tests us to see how faithful we will be in the little. God does not promote lazy people. He is looking for people who have had laziness broken from their lives.

Unforgiveness

Believe it or not, unforgiveness is one of the biggest problems the church faces today. The spirit of offense is very strong within the Christian community. Satan is working overtime to create divisions, offenses, and opportunities to walk in unforgiveness. In fact, most Christians don't handle offenses correctly. There is a biblical way to handle offenses. Even so, many Christians are not obeying what God has taught in His Word. When someone offends us, what is the proper response?

Matthew 18:15-17
Moreover if thy brother shall trespass against thee, go and tell him his fault between thee and him alone: if he shall hear thee, thou hast gained thy brother. But if he will not hear thee, then take with thee one or two more, that in the mouth of two or three witnesses every word may be established. And if he shall neglect to hear them, tell it unto the church: but if he neglect to hear the church, let him be unto thee as a heathen man and a publican.

When someone has offended us we are supposed to first go to them alone to discuss it. We are not supposed to go to other people, even our pastor, to discuss it until we have first gone to the person we have an issue with. Then, if they refuse to hear you, you are supposed to take one or two witnesses with you to discuss it. Lastly, if they still don't listen, you are supposed to take the issue before the church. Yet, what we see happening in the church is much different than what

God teaches us to do. We see people holding secret grudges, but they have not talked to the person that they believe hurt them. The sad thing is that the relationship may not be restored unless the offense is openly talked about. People have left our church in offense at times, but they never told anyone what they were offended by, and we didn't get an opportunity to work it out with them. It's very sad, really, to see what the devil has done to churches by creating offenses. In some cases, the offenses are not even real. They are merely perceived to be real. When I have had offenses in the past and talked to the person, I have learned that sometimes it's just a misunderstanding or I only had partial information. Truth is always revealed by bringing things to the light.

The real danger of unforgiveness is not towards the person who offended us, but in ourselves. When we don't forgive people or allow people to be forgiven, then we are putting ourselves in bondage. I believe that many sicknesses and infirmities of the body are tied to unforgiveness. I see unforgiveness as a disease that grows into worse things such as resentment, bitterness, depression, and even death if left to its devices. God must remove all unforgiveness from our lives, not only so we can be free from curses, but also so God can forgive us our sins. The Bible teaches us in Mark 11:26 that if we don't forgive others, God will not forgive us of our sins. When God breaks us, He is in a sense chastising us. In that chastisement, He is showing us what is like Him and what is not like Him. Unforgiveness cannot exist in the life of the believer. We are not able to be used by God or even hear His voice unless we repent of it.

False Doctrines

There are so many teachings, books, and doctrines of men that are followed by believers. The problem is that many of them are contrary to God's Word. Christians are sometimes quick to believe things that they should instead reject. The gift of discernment is needed today, because there is a lot of error taught in the church. Although books are great supplemental tools to the Bible, they should never be contrary to the Word of God. Doctrines of men sometime take us into things that are borderline witchcraft. We must have a relationship with God and know His Word in order to protect ourselves from following false doctrines of men.

I know in many charismatic circles I have seen people come up with new doctrines or revelations for people to follow as they tour churches across the nation. If we unknowingly practice or follow a false doctrine, it can stop us from fully knowing God or doing His will. God will also hold us accountable for what we teach. Don't get me wrong. I am not against seminary or books. I have a Masters in Christian Leadership from a Baptist university, but I don't subscribe to all their doctrines. I often call seminary "cemetery" because of how doctrines of men kill our spirit. We cannot reject parts of the Word, because they don't fit our denominational view point. We are not to follow denominational doctrines and teachings; we are to follow the Word of God.

Some leaders are victim to doctrines of men through their denomination. Interestingly enough, there is no mention of denominations in the Bible. It is one church in many locations, but not a denomination. As an example, many denominations have done away with the gifts of the spirit. How can we fight the devil, but have no power to do so? When did God stop healing or delivering people? When did God say that only certain people can walk in the power of God? We are all called to walk in the power of God. Part of the breaking God wants to do in us, is to remove the false doctrines and teachings of men. Allow God to do that in your life. You will see things about God and the kingdom of God you have never seen before.

Unbelief

In Hebrews 11:6 we learn that without faith it is impossible to please God. That is an incredible statement, if we think about it. How many times in our lives have we lost faith or felt hopeless? For myself, I have struggled with my faith countless times in my life. Faith is so essential to every believer's walk with God. Without faith, not only do we not please God, but we also struggle to walk in obedience to God. This past two years, I have been under so much attack in my life. I believe that God has been not only testing me, but also breaking me so that I am more usable to Him for His work.

The Lord knows our hearts. He knows when we are walking in faith and when we are walking in unbelief. Part of the breaking process is to produce new faith. This is faith we would not have had if we had not been tested or endured adversity. When we suffer adversity, we are forced to exercise our spiritual muscles of faith. Just as in the natural, if we don't work our body muscles regularly, they become weak. Suffering, tests, and trials are the gym tools that God uses to build up our faith. We learn not to trust our natural man any more. We learn that not everything is as it appears. We learn that we can no longer do things in our own strength any more. We learn we need God for everything in our lives. Without God we can do nothing. When we get to this place in our walk, we begin to believe for things that only God can do. We begin to believe for impossible things.

Mark 9:23
Jesus said unto him, If thou canst believe, all things are possible to him that believeth.

If God does not allow us to be broken, then our faith will remain at the same level that it is today. We are not going to be effective in the Kingdom of God unless we learn to work with God instead of against Him. When we walk in faith, we are agreeing with God and walking with Him in agreement. When we walk in unbelief, we are aligning ourselves with Satan and separating ourselves from God. A lot of people are running away from God, because they don't want to suffer hardship or go through anything. The reality is that you can never out run God. Jonah tried that and we see how that worked out for him. We must submit to the breaking process and allow God to grow our faith.

Fear of Man

The enemy is controlling people today through two spirits. The first one is fear of people or fear of man. The second one is with a man pleasing spirit. Many Christians are more worried about what people think about them than they are about what God thinks about them. They fear what people will think about them, or they fear that man will reject them, so they are not obedient to God. Instead, they go out of their way to compromise what they believe to fit in or be liked by other people. We cannot please men and please God at the same time. Often times, if not the majority of the time, what people want seems to be different than what God wants for us. We have to choose who we will serve. We cannot serve man and serve God. There can only be one master. I have witnessed people in ministry who are so afraid of people that they will not speak or preach truth. They would rather sugar-coat the gospel or stay away from certain topics rather than risk displeasing people. These ministers often become hirelings. They do what the people want versus what God requires. In the end, we will be held accountable for our decisions. We cannot blame other people for our disobedience. We choose to obey or disobey.

I am reminded of Saul. The Lord had instructed him to go and kill the Amalek people and all their animals. Yet, Saul disobeyed God and kept the king as a trophy and the best animals for his possession. He clearly disobeyed the command of the Lord. When the prophet Samuel confronts him for his disobedience, Saul is full of excuses. One of those excuses is that he was afraid of the people in his army. Sometimes, we use the fear of people as an excuse for our disobedience to God. The Lord will call us on that. He will not allow fear of people to affect our level of obedience. If that is the case in your life, believe me God will deal with it. He may even allow you to suffer or be broken to get you to the point where you realize you cannot rely on other people.

He did that with Job. His own family members and friends became insensitive, unloving, and uncaring in his time of trouble. All Job had was God. Of course, we know God is all any of us really need in the time of adversity. God is the one who rescues us. When we obey God, we are showing Him that we love Him above all men. When we cannot say no to people, we are walking in disobedience to the Father. We must choose whether we will serve God or we will serve those in our lives, because we cannot have two masters. That does not mean that we will not be called to serve others, but it means that we will obey God's commands even if it means upsetting or disappointing others.

CHAPTER 5

Total Surrender

There are countless numbers of people who give their lives to Christ and profess to make Him Lord and Savior. However, how many of us have been willing to lose ourselves if necessary to become like Him? Many say that they love God, but the word "love" has been overused and may mean something different depending who is saying it. Man's definition or understanding of love is different than God's definition. According to the Bible, to love God is to hate sin, and to lay down our own desires to walk in complete obedience to Him no matter what it costs us. God looks more at the heart than He does what we say. He looks for complete obedience in every area. Many people only obey God in a few areas, walking in disobedience in other areas. God is always working on men's hearts. David was known for his heart towards God. He sinned a whole lot even to the point of committing adultery and stealing a man's wife, yet God says that he was a man after His own heart. David was always quick to repentance. He was continually asking God to search his heart to see if there be any wicked thing in him.

God is looking for a people that have His heart and are willing to allow God to change their heart so they can be used by Him.

Matthew 15:8
This people draweth nigh unto me with their mouth, and honoureth me with their lips; but their heart is far from me.

Psalm 139:23-24
Search me, O God, and know my heart: try me, and know my thoughts: And see if there be any wicked way in me, and lead me in the way everlasting.

Part of the process of brokenness is surrendering our hearts, minds, and lives to Christ. When I think of the word "surrender," many things come to mind. First, I have to give up or put my hands up to someone that is more powerful than myself. When I was child, I played cops and robbers and cowboys and Indians with my brother. Whenever my brother and I played these games, one party would have to surrender to the other in order for there to be a clear winner. When it comes to serving God, sometimes our flesh can become a big obstacle to our walk with Him. Instead of surrendering to the will of God, often our flesh causes us to rebel or run away from God. Our flesh is influenced by things in our heart. If our hearts are full of evil, we will naturally do evil things; but if our hearts are fully surrendered to God, we will do godly things. Our hearts directly reflect our spiritual walk. When we talk about surrendering to God, we are talking about surrendering every area of our heart to God. He is constantly searching our hearts to see what is not like Him. We often are in denial of the things that are in our hearts. Most of us are not really honest with ourselves and don't want to see the evil that we have in our hearts. It is easier to see the sin in our brother or sister than it is to see it in ourselves. Thankfully, God is very merciful, loving, and patient with His children. Long before we see the sin in our hearts, God has already seen it. He waits patiently for His church to stop running from Him and to come back to Him. Many people initially give their lives to Christ, but then forsake God later.

Revelation 2:4
Nevertheless I have somewhat against thee, because thou hast left thy first love.

The Bible says that in the last days there will be people in the church leaving God or not loving Him as they once did. Even the very elect will be deceived by the spirit of the antichrist. I know many people that are praying and believing for revival in the church. True revival will not come until the church repents and turns back to God. God wants to be the first and only love of the church. Many people are not close to God any more. They have not fully surrendered all areas of their lives. The word refers to this type of Christian as lukewarm, not hot or cold. We cannot have one foot in the church and one foot in the world. God requires total surrender to Him. As you read this book, my prayer is that you will ask God to show you any areas of your life or in your heart that you have not fully surrendered to Him.

CHAPTER 6

Giving Control to God

*C*ontrol is a word that usually has a negative feeling to it. Most people hate it when other people control them. Sadly, we see the spirit of control in families, businesses, and in churches. There are many controlling family members, spouses, business leaders, and pastors. For myself, I am very careful not to be around controlling people. I have had people in my life that have controlled me in the past. In fact, I am very cautious not to allow people to do that to me again. That does not mean I don't love people, or that I am not under authority, or that I don't take direction form others. I believe that I am to be a man under authority and should have a teachable spirit. I also believe that we are to be accountable one to another.

One of the issues I had to deal with in my own life was a rebellious spirit. When others reject us, or hurt us, it is natural for us to want to go into self-protection mode, or to blame others. We have to be careful to repent of any unforgiveness and rebellion that may try to come upon us. We must put ourselves back into submission to God and the leaders He puts in our lives. As we were talking about the horse that needs to be broken earlier, part of the breaking process is when that horse finally gets to a place of relinquishing control of its own life to the person breaking them. We must do that with God. We must get to the point where it is no longer my way but God's way. It is no longer my will be done, but the will of the Father be done. My agendas, my way of thinking, my way of doing is now surrendered to God.

We talked about surrender last chapter, but part of surrender is relinquishing the control of our lives to God. *God, you can take me anywhere you want to go. I will obey no matter what the cost is or where you take me. I love you so much God that you can do as you please with my life. I trust you so much Lord that I will no longer hinder the work you are doing in my life. I will step aside Lord and allow you to do whatever it is you want to do in me and through me.* That is when we have given the keys to the car to the Father. We are no longer in the driver's seat. God is now driving the car. He is taking us places we may not have been willing to go before. He is doing things we may not have allowed Him to do before.

John 21:18
Truly, truly, I say to you, when you were younger, you used to gird yourself and walk wherever you wished; but when you grow old, you will stretch out your hands and someone else will gird you, and bring you where you do not wish to go

CHAPTER 7

Dying to Self

*D*eath is a word that comes to mind when I think about brokenness. It is usually a word that people don't want to think about, because it implies something coming to an end. One area that death must come to is our flesh. Part of the breaking process is dealing with our flesh also known as our sinful nature. We were all born with a sinful nature. It is the default nature that we receive as we enter into this world. The sinful nature is a powerful pull or influence in every person's life. It is often contrary to the word of God or God's nature. Because of this, there is a war in every believer's life between our sinful nature and God's nature. Part of the salvation experience is defeating the sinful nature so that we are better able to walk in obedience to God's word. In order for this to happen we have to die to the sinful nature, which means that part of us has to literally be killed in us. This is a painful process for sure, because the flesh does not die easily. In fact, my flesh has feelings, desires, and is often unruly.

So, what does it mean to die to yourself? How does this happen? What does the process look like? When we say die to our self, it means that we are dying to everything of the flesh that is in our life. Our way of thinking, the things we do, the sinful ways of our heart, the things we look at, the life we live that is contrary to God, and even the choices we make. The death process is so complete, that you will literally lose your identity and your sense of who you thought you were before you were broken. Yet, when God is finished you will have a new identity in Him. If you are like me, it is a painful process to die to self. Your flesh will not like it. The things you used to get away with, you no longer get away with any more. God will be dealing with your heart at a much deeper level than He did in the past.

Because God wants to be Lord of your life, He will take you to a place of complete dependence on Him. You will not be able to make even basic decisions about your life any more without going to the Father to ask for His direction. You are literally not your own any more. You belong to the Lord. You are His child and His possession. The difficult part of it is that you cannot do as you please any more. What you desire and what you prefer is secondary to what God wants in your life. You are no longer in control. You are no longer in the driver's seat. That does not mean that God does not want to bless you. On the contrary, God wants better for you than you want for yourself. That is why He is breaking you so that He can openly bless you. As we die to ourselves, we become more like our Father and less like our old man. His desires become our desires. His ways become our ways.

I remember several years ago when the Lord took me in the spirit to a graveyard. There I saw a freshly dug burial plot. Then I saw a casket being lowered into the ground. I asked the Lord what this was and He said just watch and listen. He instructed me to pick up a shovel and to put dirt on the casket until it was completely buried. I did not know what God was asking me to do, but I did it. After the casket was completely covered by dirt, the Lord spoke to me and said to say goodbye to the person who was in there. I asked the Lord, "Who is this person?" His response startled me. He told me to look at the grave stone. As I stared at this grave stone, I saw the name and it brought me to tears. It read, "Michael Bacon." I cried as the Lord said that I was the one in the casket, that it was me that I was burying. He told me that I needed to leave my old man in that burial plot and follow Him. He also told me that whenever my flesh tried to resurrect itself or come back that I needed to go to that burial plot and remember that I am dead. He told me to do this as often as I needed to so that I would stay dead. All of us will come to a place where we must decrease so He can increase. As long as our flesh is alive, we are no good to God. We must die to ourselves and our fleshly desires so that He can use us as an instrument of His righteousness.

CHAPTER **8**

The Purpose of Captivity

*D*uring seasons of tests and trials, God often leads us into seasons of captivity. Just as I described in my previous example about horses, each horse is taken out of their natural habitat and put in a corral. That corral represents the captivity that each of us enter into when God decides to break us. Not only are we in a strange place we have never been in before, but now we are also facing circumstances we have never encountered before. For all intents and purposes, we are imprisoned with no way out. Don't think it's strange if God chooses to put you into captivity. Many people in the Bible were put into captivity in order for God to complete the work He started in their lives. In many cases, we see that God's people were led into seasons of forced captivity and even were enslaved by their enemies.

One example of this was Joseph. God gave Joseph a dream and showed him a glimpse of his future. In the dream his brothers bowed before him. Little did Joseph know, but in order to reach the full potential that God had for his life, he would have to go through

49

more than one period of captivity in his life. I cannot imagine what Joseph must have been thinking when his brothers sold him into slavery. It had to be hard to leave his father's house where he was the favorite child to serve as a slave, especially after having a dream that seemed to mean that he would be a ruler. Not only did he serve as a slave, he later was imprisoned for crimes he did not commit. In the scheme of things, it would appear that Joseph was forsaken by his family and by God. In reality, God had a plan for Joseph's life. In fact, Joseph was later promoted to second in command in all of Egypt. Because of the blessing on his life, all of Israel was blessed and spared from famine. We also see this in the Israelites. They were God's people, yet they had to go through many periods of captivity where their enemies ruled and reigned over them and even enslaved them for periods of time.

There are seasons where God allows the enemy to put us into captivity. However, just because we go into captivity does not mean that we have sinned or are being punished. Actually, captivity has a bigger purpose in our lives then we really even know. Captivity is the beginning of the breaking process that every believer has to go through in order to be formed into what God needs us to be in order to be fit for service. It is the means by which we become imprisoned for the purpose of God. As a prisoner, we are no longer free to go where we want to or to do what we want to do. We have been imprisoned, often, against our will. Like all prison experiences, these seasons can involve hardship, lack, and persecution. They are not necessarily times of rest or peace. Captivity forces us to stand still long enough to deal with some things that we have most likely refused to deal with. I am sure Joseph had many hours, days, weeks, and months for God to work in his heart and to prepare him for his future work.

When we are in captivity we have two choices. We can either cooperate with God or we can fight against Him. If we choose to fight against God, or not submit to the breaking process, we will need to count the costs. We could miss out on what God has for us or we may even have to go back through another breaking experience until we learn to cooperate with God. If we choose to cooperate with God and let captivity do the work it needs to do in our lives, then we will come to a place of preparation where we will pass the tests we need to pass in order to go into what God has for our lives. One thing I love about Joseph is that he was still faithful to God as a slave and in prison. He walked uprightly and refused to sleep with Potiphar's wife. He walked with integrity when no one was looking. Then, in prison, he did not rebel or fight against authority. He was promoted in prison to be in charge of all the other prisoners. Then he ministered to two men who had dreams by interpreting their dreams. Later, God used this to allow Joseph to interpret Pharaoh's dream. Again, he was promoted, but, this time, he was promoted to second in command over all Egypt to oversee the preparation for a famine.

Whenever we are in captivity, we need to understand that there is a purpose for that captivity. Often times, God uses our captivity as an instrument to promote us or position us to be blessed. If it had not been for the captivity or imprisonment, we may not have been ready for the blessing that God has for our lives. When I think about all the times I was in periods of captivity, I remember the many lessons I learned. Some of these lessons were: the value of waiting on God, patience, faith, trust, forgiveness, obedience, and humility. I had to learn that God was my Source, Provider, Protector, Healer, and Deliverer. Had it not been for the seasons of trials, tests, tribulations, and brokenness, I would not be where I am today serving God. The captivity was a necessary work in order to prepare me for what God had in store for my life.

Maybe you are reading this book and you are in a period of captivity. You are in a place requiring total surrender. There is no way out this time, other than waiting on the Lord to do it. Allow God to finish the work He has started in you. Instead of fighting against the process or going against the grain, go with the flow of His Spirit and allow yourself to be broken so God can build you back up to who He has called you to be. Start today by stopping the wrestling match with God. He will perform the work He started in you. He is faithful to complete that good and perfect work in you.

CHAPTER 9

The Purpose of Delays

*F*irst, let me say that I am not naturally a patient person. I usually want things to get done immediately and don't like to wait around for long. My flesh, by nature, has a very short attention span. In fact, there are certain retailers that I avoid at all costs because I don't like waiting in lines. I am the same way driving cars. I hate traffic jams, and I would rather take open highways that are longer distance than to wait in heavy traffic. Unfortunately, when I am praying and asking God for something, I am the exact same way. I want what I want yesterday. I get frustrated at times with God, because it seems my timeline and His timeline simply don't match. When I pray, I am thinking it will happen immediately in my situation, but God often has a different timeline in mind. At times, my flesh gives me fits because of the waiting or delays. I know what the Bible says concerning waiting, and I know that I need to wait upon the Lord, but my flesh wants it now. I know I am not the only person out there like this. I know many people that battle with their patience.

One of the challenges I have had as a believer is that when the Lord chooses to take me into a breaking season, more than likely it will require a period of waiting on the Lord or several delays in receiving my breakthrough. This often tests my faith and my mood. I can get irritable, angry, depressed, or anxious. I can also lose my peace if I don't remind myself that God is in control. Usually when there is delay the devil is in my face by orchestrating events or attacks against me. It's often hard to understand why God would allow the devil to attack us. We forget the bigger picture or the plans that He has to prosper us, because we are neck deep in spiritual or physical warfare. I have seen so many Christians who have fallen away from the Lord, because they have grown weary in waiting on God. They have lost hope, because it seems the breaking season was so long with no breakthrough in sight.

The enemy often convinces Christians that God has forgotten them or has failed them. Satan will tell us that we must have done something wrong for God not to bless us or that we are being punished by God. We cannot listen to the devil during times of breaking or delay. He is a liar and a deceiver. His plans are to kill, steal, and destroy. The truth is that most of the time it is the enemy trying to stop our blessings. Satan uses people and circumstances to delay our breakthrough. Oddly, God allows these delays as part of His plan to work out our salvation and our spiritual growth. I love how the Lord lets the devil think he is winning, when in reality he is playing right into the hands of God. The Lord is even using the delays to perfect the church.

When delays happen, it tests our faith, our patience, our trust in God. We find out whether we have passed the test or not. We learn whether there is more breaking that needs to done, or whether we are ready to graduate to the next level in God. For myself, I have had many internal struggles that I have had to fight. I have had to overcome wrong thinking, sin, and anger when my blessings have been delayed. In my case, I used to be like a little baby when things did not go my way. As I have matured over the years, I am less and less angry and have even laughed about delays when they happen because I now realize that delays are part of my breaking process and often, the final test before passing the exam. A test to see if I am ready to be released into what God has for me to do or not. If you are at a place where you are having major delays, it simply means you're almost there. However, I will warn you that "almost there" can mean different things to different people in different seasons of their lives. For some of us the delays are days, weeks, months, or years. In my case, as God takes me higher, the breaking process repeats itself with much more intensity the next time around. The delays now get longer and longer.

The Bible talks about taking us from one level of glory to another level of glory. I never understood the cost of going from glory to glory. I truly did not know that it meant that I would be broken over and over again until I reached the level God wanted me to get to or that it would require tests or delays. I thought somehow I would one day graduate or stop having to experience these things, but the truth is that God is continually fine-tuning us and making us ready for the next move or work He has for us to do. This is an ongoing process until the day we die. If we love God, we are not exempt from this process. He wants to use all of us for His work, which means we must all die to ourselves, submit to being broken, and put up with the delays that come with the process. We must overcome our tendencies to give up, get angry, or take matters into our own hands. We must learn to submit to the working that happens through these delays.

There are aspects to delays that I never considered before. For example, delay is not denial. Just because there is a delay does not mean God is denying our prayer request or we are not getting our breakthrough. When we encounter delays there are a number of things that could be happening. First, the devil knows your blessing is on the way, and he is trying his best to stop it. He can try to stop it by using our own words (negative confession), setting up circumstances, or by sending demons on assignment. Second, often your blessing is on the way, but God has His angels working on assignment to set it up for your good. There are things going on during your season of delay that you are unaware of. God is working it out for your good, but you cannot see it yet. For example, someone instrumental in your blessing has to be obedient to release it or you have not talked to the right person that God has granted you favor with. Third, God allows delay to further break you down.

Delay can really be discouraging. People have different reactions to delays, but think about these things:

1. Will we lose our peace?
2. Will we ruin our testimony?
3. Will we take things into our own hands and create an Ishmael?
4. Will we continue to praise God in our storms?

5. Will we continue to speak words of faith or speak negativity?
6. Will we be obedient to God even though we cannot see our blessing yet?
7. Will we curse God or continue to pray and believe?
8. Will we fall away or continue to stand strong?

If you are experiencing delay, then it is many times evidence of a greater work happening. God has a plan for your life. He is allowing delays as part of your breaking process to show your heart or issues with your faith or some other area of your walk. Trust God and let Him use these delays to complete the work He has begun in your life. In the end, you will inherit the blessing God has promised; and, when you do, you will be ready for the next move of God.

CHAPTER 10

Trusting God

*T*rust is something that many people battle with. I believe this to be true, because I have witnessed so many Christians who question whether God loves them when they are going through a test, trial or breaking period. I have seen the pain and anguish that the breaking process can produce in peoples' lives. When the attacks come there is a shift from faith to fear and even anger. If we trust God, should we not trust Him both in the good times and the bad times? Do we only believe God loves us when things are going well, or should we believe that God loves us no matter what is happening in our lives? Even bigger, do we only love God when we are blessed and walking in favor, or do we love God even when we are being disciplined, broken, or going through hardships? When we say we trust someone, it means that we believe that they are a person of their word. That they mean what they say. We believe that this person has our back in times of trouble. We believe that the person will be there when we need them to be. We also believe that the person has the best intentions towards us. When it comes to

God, He loves us so much. He has plans to prosper us. His goal is not to hurt us, but to bless us. If we truly believe God, then we must trust Him at all costs; yet, most Christians I know have a hard time trusting other people and trusting God.

There are people we trust to a degree, but we would not trust with our life. There are a few people that we may trust with our very lives. With God, we have to trust Him in every area of our lives. We must give Him complete control of our life. We cannot pick and choose which areas we will believe God in. We must trust Him in all things. We must give Him our full heart, our life, our family, our ministry, our health, our finances, and our future. This means that we trust God to do what is best for us even when the storms of life come, or breaking comes – that we know that He will take care of us. We may go through some difficult times, but we trust God to redeem us from every curse. There are many people that only trust God with certain areas of their lives. To demonstrate our trust, we must take our hands off of our situations. We can no longer be in control. We have to give control of our life back to the Lord.

One of the reasons that people have trust issues is that they have had bad experiences in their lives where someone they trusted let them down. Maybe your parent was not a good parent and did not take care of you or keep their word. Perhaps your spouse or another family member betrayed you or did not do what they said they would. Because of past experiences where someone in your life that was close to you broke confidence or did not keep their commitment, you now have a problem trusting other people or even trusting God. This is especially true for children who have been abandoned by their parents or who were unwanted by their family. They have learned to do everything for themselves and feel they cannot trust anyone else to take care of them or love them. In some cases, we need inner healing and need to be delivered before we can fully trust God. Some of us may even need to forgive other people who have hurt us, betrayed us, cursed us, or broken their promises to us. Satan would love to create distrust between believers and church leaders as well. For example, you were hurt by a pastor or church leader, so now you don't trust other pastors. Once we become distrusting of others, we tend to operate in a spirit of control to protect ourselves. We learn to only trust ourselves to take care of things in our lives. However, this is a major issue because we must die to ourselves, which means we can no longer be in control of our lives. We must give that control back to the Lord. We also must allow God to use other people in our lives to help us. If we don't trust God or the leaders He puts in place, we are preventing ourselves from getting the breakthrough that we need. Trust opens the door to God's provision. Faith comes by hearing the Word of God. If we don't trust God to perform His Word, we are walking in unbelief. If God promises something to us, He will do what He says He will do as long as we believe it and trust Him to do it. Distrust and unbelief go hand-in-hand. Trust and faith go hand-in-hand. To trust is to believe.

Chapter 11

God's Breaking in My Own Life

*M*y life has not been an easy one to live. I know that everyone probably feels that way, but in my case, I feel like I have been broken time and time again. It has felt like a continual and repeated process in my life. At times, the attacks and trials have been overwhelming in my life. I have wondered at times "why?" It could be that I am very stubborn compared to most people, or perhaps my calling is different, but I am not exactly sure why my life has not been as easy as it has been for others. For whatever reason, it seems that God has broken me over and over again. I don't want you to think that I am complaining about my life or that I have self-pity in my heart, because I really don't feel that way at all. Instead, I believe that God has allowed me to be broken and rebroken for a greater purpose. There is not one wasted year, month, or day of my life. God has truly used everything for my good, just as He has in so many other people's lives. Yet, I know that some people are broken more often and for longer periods of time than other people. The same is true in the analogy of horses we talked about earlier. Some horses are more stubborn than others and require additional breaking. Other horses are being broken for different roles such as horseback riding, pulling wagons or carriages, or plowing fields. Depending on their purpose, they may be broken and trained differently or even require more intensive conditioning. In our lives, the greater the call, the greater the breaking is going to be.

As a brief summary, I did not have the best life growing up, and I suffered many hurts and rejections. I was a person with very little hope growing up. I felt very unloved and unappreciated by others. I will not dredge up all the gory details, but I thank God that I can forgive and learn from all that I went through. I will for a moment talk about the events that led up to my salvation. Since I felt so unloved growing up, I thought that life was about finding a woman that would love me. That, of course, was not what life was about. A person can never take the place of God. The void of love that we have in our life can only be filled by God. A spouse is an added compliment to the love of God, but can never can take His place.

Leading up to my salvation there were a series of events tied to rejection. In addition to my childhood pain, I enlisted in the armed forces and lived overseas. I had found a military woman that I thought I would marry. She, like me, was a very hurt person and had many problems. Something awful had happened to her growing up. It was so bad that she would never share it with me. One day, I had this thought come to my mind – that she had been raped. I asked her, and she went crazy, screamed, yelled, and cried hysterically.

Our relationship was never the same afterwards. She eventually left me for someone else. I felt rejected all over again and hit a low point in my life.

Feeling unloved, unwanted, and alone again, I decided that I would end my life by suicide. I did not have a relationship with God at this time, but all through my childhood I would pray and talk to the invisible God I had never met. My prayers as a child were abnormal compared to how other kids pray. My daily prayer was that God would kill me. I kept this secret from my family. They really never knew the extent of the pain I was in or how depressed I was with my life. Some of it was caused by life experiences, but some of it was my unforgiveness towards others. I saw death as a way out of the pain I suffered as a child. Then, as an adult, I thought death was the only way to get rid of my pain. As I contemplated suicide, I held out hope that even in the attempt to end my life that God would somehow reveal Himself to me because I wanted something to live for.

Long story short, I picked a mountain to drive my car off to end my life. Right before driving the car off the mountain, I prayed that God would spare my life. As I drove off the mountain, my whole life flashed in front of me. I felt so much fear, and I knew then I did not want to die. Death was not an escape for me. It was just a trick to take me away prematurely. In the end, God did spare my life. My car was totaled, but I did not have a scratch on my body. God showed me love and spared me from death. I gave my life to Jesus that day and started to attend church.

I thought somehow that, once I had Jesus in my life, things would become a whole lot easier. The first year or so I felt very joyful and hopeful, but then God decided to go deeper into my heart and life to bring about changes that I can only describe as very painful to deal with. God had a plan for my life, but my flesh was still in full operation. The breaking process began in my life. God allowed me to sin, and also to make a lot of mistakes. My walk with God was not like someone that was raised in the church. I was hardheaded and sinful. I was lukewarm for many years. I had a deep love for God, but I was still full of hurt and unforgiveness, and I suffered from rejection and self-esteem issues. I kept looking for love in the wrong places or thinking the love of a person would fix the big hole in my heart. Jesus should have been enough, but the pain in me was not dealt with yet.

One thing that I have learned in my life is that when you think the breaking season is over, another season of breaking will come. He will give you time to rest, and then He will say, "Okay, we have another layer of things to deal with." For me, I had to be broken of many things that included pride, lust, rejection, betrayal, unforgiveness, fear of man, anger, judgments, rebellion, and laziness. Often times, it was circumstances that taught me the most. I learned things about myself that only God could show me through these circumstances. Some of the circumstances God used to break me were things like divorce, job layoff, personal betrayals, and failed business opportunities.

Divorce was one of the biggest breakings that has ever happened in my life. It literally was like going through a death process. The person you were married to now decides that they don't love you, so they have an affair with someone else. Only, you are left to pick up the pieces of your life. On the surface, you want to feel sorry for yourself and maybe others will too, because the person cheated on you and left you all alone. The reality is that many people cannot relate to the pain you experience.

I remember when my first wife left me. I was not just getting divorced – I became a full-time, single dad of four children. I had a double whammy to deal with. Raising four children was not easy to say the least. To be fair, I had been a hard husband to live with. I thought the wife should do everything. I found myself doing laundry, cooking meals, changing diapers, and caring for sick children by myself.

There was one point that I wanted to walk out the door. My children were all sick with a stomach virus. They were taking turns vomiting; and because I have a weak stomach, I was taking turns vomiting with them. I wanted to run out of the house. I wanted to call my ex-wife and ask her to come pick the kids up. It was a stressful time. I had no washing machine or dryer, so I had to wash the clothes by hand and hang up the clothes on the clothes hanger out back of my apartment. I had no life really, other than church. Two of my four kids were in diapers. I had my hands full and did not have a clue how to parent them. All my finances were going to daycare. I was living pay check to pay check. I will tell you, though, that God used this situation to give me a love for my children and a respect for women. I was learning first-hand what it was like being in a woman's shoes, a single mother to be exact. My son saw me as mom and dad, and at one point he called me "Mommy Daddy" regularly. That was my name to him – "Mommy Daddy."

I wish that I could say that I learned all I needed to during this time. However, there was apparently still more God had to break in my life. I soon remarried, and much too soon to be honest. It was a year-and-a-half later, and I was married again, this time to someone that I did not really know. She said she was Christian. I took her word for it. I married for the wrong reasons. I just wanted someone to love me. Even after marriage, I still felt unloved and rejected most times. I had a problem looking for the wrong kind of women to be honest. I am not making excuses, but I was not raised in the church and I was still battling some serious issues. So, even after three prophets told me not to marry my second wife, I proceeded to marry her anyway. It was a nightmare from day one. Why? It was not a God-ordained marriage but, instead, an Ishmael type experience. I made that marriage happen instead of waiting for the woman God wanted me to have. I honestly believe God allowed me to reap what I had sown, which was disobedience.

To cut to the chase, the second marriage was very difficult. We made it to the seven-year mark just like my first marriage. Like the first marriage, my second wife had an affair. This time the damage was not just to me, but also to my children. By then, I wanted to give up on God, on church, and even on women. I was not very godly during the time of separation, and I will be honest and say that I could have easily fallen completely back into the world had it not been for a God-encounter that happened to me. God spoke audibly to me for the first time and ministered to me. I felt the flood of God's love for the first time in several years. God began healing me, my heart, and my life. It was during this time that

God also said to me that when I felt qualified I was unqualified to be used by Him. Now that I was broken, He could finally use me.

I don't fully understand the ways of God or how He sees things. Look at David as an example. Why did God love him so much? He had an affair with a married woman and had her husband killed; yet God forgave him and still loved him. Yes, there was a season of reaping what he did wrong, but then God's love still was resident in his life. I believe that Satan thinks that, if he can get us to mess up or get someone else to mess us over, that we will be no use for God and most likely give up on being a Christian. What God has taught me is that He uses flawed people, and if we truly repent and turn our lives over to Him fully, He can still make something out of our lives.

Over thirteen years ago, God brought me a woman that would love me like I had never been loved before by a person. Now I want to also say that one of the lessons God taught me through divorce is that God is my first love. No person can take His place, but He can give you someone that will love you the way you should be loved. We have had a wonderful marriage, although at times we've had to fasten our seat belts and hold on for our dear lives. Attacks have been strong against us. Yet, what a blessing it has been.

I don't know why, but even out of all that sin and breaking, God chose to use my wife and me to go into ministry. It was after our hearts were healed and as we finally surrendered to the call. And, God has used us despite of our imperfections or past mistakes. However, a majority of the tests, trials, attacks, and brokenness we experienced later came from being in ministry. Let us just say that you cannot be unforgiving and be a pastor. You cannot get upset when people reject you in ministry, because it will happen a lot. People will gossip about you, walk out on you, stab you in the back, or even lie about you. All the years I went through rejection and betrayal certainly have helped me in ministry; however, even then, it was not enough to fully prepare me. Brokenness has been a common theme for us in ministry. No one really knows what pastors endure. It is one of the hardest roles I have ever had in my life. Although we have had many loving relationships in ministry there have also been some attacks through some others. I have had to learn to love people no matter what they do or say to me or my family. I have had to endure long periods of time where I did not see growth. I have had to stand alone in many situations. Only a broken man can fully depend on God.

In my case, it has not just been ministry that God has used to break me, but I have also had to work a secular job. He has used jobs and periods of no jobs to break me. Until recently, I was laid off from a very high paying job. I was unemployed for over twenty-two months. I could hardly even get an interview anywhere. No one would hire me. This was the first time in my life that I could not get work. It affected not just me and my family, but it also affected our church; because we were no longer tithing due to the lack of income. Now, even though this was a major breaking, God was still providing for us supernaturally in these twenty-two months. I can tell you that we never missed a bill or our mortgage in over twenty-two months. God made a way for us in some of the most unusual ways. The government actually paid our mortgage for over eighteen of those months. Then, after the last mortgage payment was paid, I was offered a job out of state. I initially accepted that offer, because I felt I had no choice. That was when the Holy Spirit reminded me of what He taught me over the past few years. Through my breaking, I have learned to trust God in everything. I now know that I work for God and not man. I know that I must do things God's way not my way. I would have not known that if I had not been broken. I was at a point when I accepted this job that I had put the church in His hands. I had also put our house and future in His hands. As hard as it was, I felt I could not abandon the church and ministry we had started in North Carolina unless God told me to, and He had not instructed me to do that. I called the company where I had accepted the job and told them I was sorry, but I could not come after all. Then an interesting thing happened. The same company called back and asked me if I would be willing to work from home so that I would not have to move.

God has not only broken us the past few years, but He has shown Himself to be true as our provider. Now, even as I write this book, God has used the brokenness in my life to create a dependence on Him. I am at a place now of total surrender. I no longer run from situations that are meant to break me. I have given myself over to God and learned that my life is not my own. It is no longer I who live but Christ who lives within me. I may not look like the typical pastor or leader in the body of Christ, because my past is full of mistakes; but I am an example of what God can do when a man finally surrenders himself to Christ. Brokenness is part of God's process of preparing us for greater.

Chapter 12

You Must Lose Your Life to Save It

God has a plan for every person's life. Most people don't really understand how much God loves His people. I believe Adam and Eve also struggled with this understanding. When they sinned against God, one of the first things they did was hide from God and cover themselves. The spirit of shame is powerful, and the enemy uses it to chase us away from God. The Lord loves us so much – not just when we are perfect, but even when we sin against Him. He certainly hates the sin, but He loves us unconditionally. He is loving, kind, merciful, and long suffering, probably much more than we can comprehend in our natural minds. If only people really understood how much He loves them!

For me personally, it was not until this past year that I finally accepted the fact that God still loves me even when I make mistakes. Previously, I could believe that God loves everyone else; but, for myself, I felt unworthy of that love. Because I did not feel that God could love me, I could not bring myself to trust Him with my life. I was scared that God would not do something good for me but, instead, would be punished for my past mistakes. Most people don't fully trust God the way they should. This was a scheme in my life for many years until I was set free. As part of the spiritual breaking in my life, the Lord took me through situations and seasons where I could no longer trust myself, but instead I had to trust God to get through them.

I know many of you reading this book are most likely battling trust issues as well. When we let go of our lives and trust God with the outcomes we are always in a better situation than taking matters into our own hands. Just like the horses that get caught, corralled, and harnessed, we too need to submit to be broken and trained. We must be conformed to the Word of God and learn to wait on the Lord. When we learn to stand still and wait on the salvation of the Lord, God is always on time.

I have learned so many things these past few years, but one of the biggest is that our life does not belong to us. We belong to the Lord, and He can do with us as He pleases. We must cooperate with the working of the Holy Spirit in order to walk in the blessings of God. When we are where we need to be, doing what we are called to do, then the blessings will chase after us. It begins with brokenness, but it continues through our obedience to the Father.

CHAPTER 13

Broken for a Purpose

*W*hen I hear the word "broken," I think of something being shattered or in pieces. To be honest the word does not even sound good to me. No one likes to be broken. Our flesh hates the word and the process that brokenness requires. We are the clay in the Potter's hands. When the Father is through with us, we will be the vessel He has called us to be. Even the Potter has times where the clay does not fully cooperate, so He has to start over again to reshape the clay to be the vessel He wants it to be. In the end, the Potter takes what He sees in his own mind and turns the lump of clay into something beautiful. Only, that is not the end of the process. That shaped clay that had to be bent and molded into a vessel, now has to be put into a fiery furnace to be baked.

Breaking is not just the bending and molding God has to do in our lives. It also involves the fiery trials and tests that we must endure. The breaking process includes periods of isolation, times of lack, times of extreme testing, periods of waiting on God, and changing our mindsets. I can look back in my life and see how God not only broke me through my circumstances, but also changed the way my mind sees things. Our minds often control our ability to behave correctly to the will of God. We cannot have carnality of the mind and expect that God will be able to use us. The Bible says that a man must not be double-minded. Double-minded men are unstable in all their ways. We must not only be broken in our life, but we have to be broken in our minds. It truly is a psychological battle. In our humanity we often allow our minds to rule and reign versus taking our thoughts into captivity as the Word of God expects us to do.

A big component to being broken is submission. When we submit to something we are submitting to a higher authority. We are submitting our life, our will, and our emotions. We are laying down our self-will, desires, and sense of direction. Imagine a horse that has not been fully broken. The rider tells the horse to go left, but, because the horse has a mind of its own and has not learned to submit to its master, the horse becomes unruly and useless to the master. We must not allow ourselves to operate in the spirits of stubbornness and rebellion. We know we are truly broken when we fully trust and obey the commands of our master. We know we are not broken when we allow our mind or emotions to dictate our lives. Many of us say we want God to use us. How many will say, "Yes Lord, no matter what the cost!" The cost is brokenness and complete surrender.

Everything that is in us that is not like God will be broken, because God has to remove that which is not like Him from our lives. I have personally witnessed how most Christians run from adversity and trials versus embracing them. I believe that, especially in America,

Christians are more or less fair-weather Christians. We will serve God, if it does not hurt us too much to do so. Once God starts messing with our mind, our will, and our emotions, many Christians don't want any part of that. In order to be used by God, I must decrease and He must increase. I can no longer be in control of my own life. A servant (broken vessel) is used for the Master's purposes. A servant does not tell the Master what to do. The Master tells the servant what to do and when to do it. The servant does not question or second guess the Master. The servant does as they are commanded to do without complaining or rebellion. We know we are broken when we no longer worry about ourselves but about being pleasing to our Father.

Conclusion

*I*n conclusion, God is not looking for slaves; instead, He is looking for children who have allowed themselves to gratefully receive the discipline of the Father. Every good parent disciplines the children that they love. God could not love us without disciplining us. Discipline is a part of the breaking process and is a gift from God. For those that are parents, there are times that our children don't understand or appreciate discipline we give them. I know at times growing up I even resented my parents when I was disciplined. I did not understand that they saw things I could not see for myself. I did not realize that the things I was receiving discipline for would help create who I am today. I love that about God. He sees things for us that we cannot see for ourselves. He also knows things about us and our future that we don't know. He loves us so much that He will discipline and break us now, so we can be blessed later. When I fully trust God, I trust Him with every aspect of my life. I don't pick and choose the areas that God can deal with. I give Him all of my life. I may at times think I am losing part of my identity or what I want to do, but, in the end, I will become who

God wants me to be. He is the Father that loves His children. He is the one that knows what is best for them.

I pray that this book has spoken to someone, that you will consider what has been taught concerning brokenness, that you will search your heart for areas where you have resisted the breaking process and allow God to complete the good work He has started in your life. God bless you, Brother or Sister in Christ, and may God finish what He has started within you, for He knows the plans He has for you, plans to prosper you.

Biography

*M*ichael Bacon is the husband of Lyn Bacon, father of eight children, and grandfather of three. Michael is Senior Pastor and Co-Founder of Glory Tabernacle International Ministries (GTIM) in Youngsville, North Carolina. He has a Master's in Christian Leadership from Liberty University and has been in ministry since 2007. He believes in the Body of Christ fulfilling the work of God and fully believes in mentorship, discipleship, as well as equipping, activating and releasing people into their ministry. The Lord has called him to an international ministry and he has ministered throughout the world. His heart call is for the continent of Africa, where he has been used to lead thousands to Christ as well as pray for many healings, and miracles such as the blind seeing, deaf hearing, and the lame walking. His main calling is apostolic in nature and he flows in the spirit through prophecy, healing and deliverance. Michael is available for travel and ministry as Holy Spirit leads. You can contact him by email at glorytabernaclenc@hotmail.com or by mail at PO Box 999, Youngsville, NC 27596. You can also view his church and speaking itinerary by going to www.rainingglory.org

CPSIA information can be obtained
at www.ICGtesting.com
Printed in the USA
LVHW081628130120
643458LV00037B/2702/P